French Lancers

French Lancers

by

Nigel de Lee

illustrated by

Emir Bukhari

ALMARK

Almark Publishing Co. Ltd., London

First Published 1976.

ISBN 0 85524 256 6

Distributed in the U. S. A. by
Squadron/Signal Publications Inc.,
3515E, Ten Mile Road,
Warren, Michigan 48091.

Printed in Great Britain by
Chapel River Press,
Weyhill Road, Andover,
Hampshire,
for the publishers, Almark Publishing Co. Ltd.
49 Malden Way, New Malden,
Surrey KT3 6EA, England.

Contents

Preface

In this book we shall examine the tactical employment of French Napoleonic Lancers. The text will cover the role of the Lancer in battle and during the advance to contact and withdrawal. The second chapter examines the way cavalry manoeuvred on and off the battle field. Though some commanding officers strove for almost parade ground precision there were sound tactical reasons behind many of the formations and movements. In action Lancers were a shock weapon that could break up enemy units and then harry them across country. However cavalry were only effective when the enemy infantry had been reduced by gun fire or when their morale was low, and some of the defeats and disasters of the Napoleonic Wars came about when unsupported cavalry were launched against steady infantry and guns.

The Lancer and his Weapons

In 1809, at the battle of Wagram, some Polish light horse in the French service took lances from a body of Austrian Uhlans and used them to good effect. Their success impressed Napoleon; for he arranged for a squadron of the 3rd Hussars to undergo experimental training with the lance, and in June 1811, six regiments of Dragoons were converted into Lancers.

These troops carried a variety of arms. Napoleon wanted them to be able to continue to act as mounted infantry, so at first each man carried a sabre, lance, carbine with bayonet, and two pistols. The troopers rapidly discarded the carbine and bayonet, and usually carried only one pistol. In 1812 the Emperor, a believer in the value of firepower in all circumstances, insisted that at least one third of each troop of Lancers should carry the carbine. By 1813 it was apparent that a rear rank armed with lances were more danger to the front rank than they were to the enemy, so rear rank troopers, N.C.O.s and officers gave up the lance for the carbine.

The Lancer also had some protection in the form of his uniform. Troopers sometimes wore leather jerkins beneath their jackets, and these with the leather cross-belts, gave fair protection against sword cuts. French cavalry often supplemented this by slinging a rolled cloak or blanket over the right shoulder and diagonally across the body. This covered the back and front, and the left kidney, usually a favourite target for the mounted pursuer. But, it could also be seized by an opponent on horse or foot and used to drag the trooper from his horse.

The tall Polish Lancer cap, the *Czapka*, gave protection against cuts to the head. For a while after their conversion, French Lancer regiments continued to wear their Dragoon helmets. These were very effective indeed, as a British officer of the 14th Light Dragoons who encountered one at Espeja in Spain in September 1811 recorded: '. . . he wore a brass helmet, and the blade of my sabre broke in two on it.'

The horse was also an indispensable part of the Lancers' equipment. It was the horse, if properly trained and well handled, which gave the Lancer the advantage over his antagonists. The mount could also be used as a weapon. In pursuit or *mêlée* the horse could use its chest to ram the flank of an enemy horse to bring it down or unbalance the rider. The animal could also be used against men on foot; at Albuhera, in May 1811, a British officer states that, having been wounded by a Lancer: '. . . the wretch tried . . . to make his horse trample on me.'

The size of the horse ridden by the Lancer varied. The Lancers of the Imperial Guard rode horses of 14¼ to 14½ hands, other formations made do with smaller ones. Larger horses were an advantage in a charge, where they provided impetus, but were less able to survive the exertions and privations of a campaign than smaller ones.

The weapons carried all had their uses, except for the bayonet which got lost at an early stage.

The pistol was most frequently used when on outpost duty, especially at night, as a signal to attract the attention of friendly forces, or raise an alarm. It was sometimes used in skirmishing, but when it was, enemy skirmishers were in little danger. The pistol could be lethal at extremely close quarters. If a Lancer got into a situation where he had no room to wield his lance and insufficient time to draw his sabre, he could snatch out his pistol and use it to dispose of an immediate enemy. On the day before Waterloo Sir Hussey Vivian observed a Lancer blowing out the brains of a British Hussar during a *mêlée* near Genappe. In flight, the pistol could be laid upon the left shoulder in order to discourage a pursuer from approaching within sword's length of the left flank. The pistol could also be used to annoy enemy infantry in square in an attempt to draw their fire; at Quatre Bras and Waterloo Lancers killed many British infantry in square with their pistols.

The carbine could be used in the same manner. It was also used for outpost duty, and was the natural weapon for skirmishing. A Colonel of the Lancers of the Guard, de Brack, optimistically reckoned the carbine to be effective at 90 metres. Unfortunately, if he wished to shoot with any degree of accuracy, a Lancer had to fire whilst his horse was still, in which case he himself was an easy target. On rare occasions Lancers would dismount and use their carbines to clear enclosures or villages; in such situations they acted as light infantry.

The sabre was carried for use at close quarters when the lance had been lost or could not be used due to lack of space. French cavalry were trained to thrust rather than cut with their swords. It was believed that an accurate and vigorous thrust was always more effective than the cut favoured by British light cavalry; that a thrust could be delivered more quickly, and would reach a man beyond the range of a cut. But, an excited man on a moving horse sometimes found it difficult to thrust accurately, and it was easier to deliver cuts than thrusts to the sides and rear.

The lance was made of ash and steel, measured nine feet in length, and weighed about four pounds. The butt was tapered and sheathed in steel; when the lance was slung it rested in a ring on the right stirrup. The head, called the 'spear', had three parts. The blade was triangular, nine inches long, and one and a quarter wide at the base. It was flat in section so as to pass easily between the ribs of a victim. (Later on in the Nineteenth Century, British lances were given blades with a diamond or triangular section, so that a wound would heal less easily). Behind the blade was a short shaft, and then a ball, intended to prevent the blade from penetrating too far. Behind the ball stretched metal strips, designed to protect the shaft from sword cuts, and to secure the banderol, a triangular or swallow tailed pennant which could be used in action to disconcert enemy horses, and was so used at Albuhera and Genappe. At the balancing point, the shaft was bound by a narrow leather strap; this provided a secure hand grip, and also secured the sling, a loop of leather some two feet long. When the lance was being carried, the sling went over the right shoulder; when the Lancer was in action, he would have the sling wound tightly around his right wrist to bind it to his weapon. On service, the lance required attention. The metal parts had to be greased against rust, the wood and leather kept clean. The shaft was sometimes distorted by the action of wind on the banderol, and sometimes it would break unexpectedly, which was inconvenient in action.

The lance was not an easy weapon to handle. The length and weight made it awkward. (In later years the British used bamboo shafts to reduce the weight of their lances, the Germans applied their customary scientific bent and made them of aluminium). Contemporary authorities agreed that the lance could only be useful in the hands of an intelligent, well trained horseman with exceptionally strong arms and hands and a good sense of balance. One French

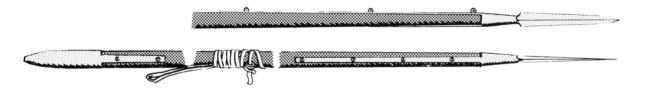

A French lance. It weighed about four pounds and was nine feet long. The butt was sheathed in steel and the point of balance had a leather loop for ease of carrying and holding. The flat blade was nine inches long.

historian, F. Masson, summed up the characteristics of the lance as follows: 'The fastest, lightest, most inspiring, effective and terrible weapon in the hands of an intelligent horseman; the slowest, heaviest, most beastly and useless in the hands of an idiot.'

In consequence, Lancers were initially trained to handle their weapon in open order on foot. Having become strong and dextrous enough to manipulate the lance safely with one hand, (the other being held as if gripping the reins of a horse), they went on to mounted training. This entailed tilting at rings and targets placed on the ground, as well as much practise of the basic movements.

There were three basic types of offensive movement to be learned by the Lancer; thrusts, parries, and cuts.

All movements were made from the basic 'Guard' position. In this, the Lancer sat on his saddle, his left hand holding the reins short so as to direct the horse's head away from the spear. The lance was held in the right hand at the point of balance, the thumb on top, the fingers encircling the shaft with the nails up. The sling bound the shaft firmly to the wrist and the forearm clamped the shaft to the right side of the body, two inches below the breast. If the enemy were mounted, the shaft would pass over the horse's head, with the point at the level of a horse's ears. If the enemy were on foot, the point would be at the level of his mount's nostril.

The Lancer was trained to thrust or 'point' in all directions. Unlike the medieval knight, who sat firm in a deep saddle, aimed his horse and himself to aim his lance, and used the momentum of his horse to push home the weapon, the Napoleonic Lancer used his right arm to thrust with his lance, as the drill instruction for 'Front, give point,' demonstrates:

'. . . half extend the arm to the rear, rise in the stirrups, lean forward . . . against cavalry, give point with force horizontally to the front, letting the lance glide along in the hand about three or four inches, passing it close to the horse's off ear; the wrist turned inwards, the shaft well closed to the right forearm, and supported firmly between it and the body . . . the point . . . if against cavalry, is aimed horizontally, or rather elevated, so as to enter a little above the waist ... against infantry, vertically to enter the breast.'

After giving point, the Lancer was to withdraw the point quickly, and return to the 'Guard' position. Attempts to perform these movements without striking the horse with spear or butt led to many injuries and accidents. Lancers suffered from sprained wrists, wrenched elbows and dislocated shoulders, and many fell or were thrown.

An inexperienced Lancer who thrust too vigorously when attempting the point against infantry might perform an involuntary pole-vault and be catapulted from his stirrups over the head of his horse which might then trample him.

The Lancer was envisaged as the centre of a circle of which his lance was the diameter, and as capable of giving a deadly thrust to any point on the circle. If he wished to point to the right, he had to twist his body in that direction, and support his lance between his forearm and his back. If he pointed to the left, he twisted leftwards, swung the lance in a horizontal semicircle over the horse's head, and rested the shaft on his left forearm, or on the elbow if he wished to cover the left flank or rear. To point to the right rear he was obliged to swing the point up in a semicircle, raising the lance over his head, change grip, lower the lance, then twist to the right rear. These movements could be very difficult; if the lance were on the left arm, it might impair control of the horse; movement of the lance itself could alarm the horse or unbalance the rider; in thrusting to the rear it was hard to maintain grip and control whilst pushing with sufficient force; and when he was looking to his rear, the lancer could not see where he was going. Perhaps the most risky movement of all was changing the direction of the lance by the 'St George'; in this, the Lancer raised the lance above his head at arms length, balanced it on his palm with hand open, and used his forefinger to twirl it until it pointed in the required direction.

The parries were horizontal movements of the lance, designed to deal with hostile cavalry who were too close or too numerous to be disposed of by thrusts. The parry was delivered from a firm seat, and used the lance as a quarterstaff. A parry could be delivered to the right or left forward quarter of the circle in which the lancer sat simply by twisting the body in the required direction. If he were surrounded by enemies and had no comrades within lance length, a Lancer could use the 'alentour parez', a full circular movement of the weapon, the point travelling from left rear to right rear in one movement and back again, the action being repeated twice. For such violent action, a firm grip was essential, as the regulations stated:

'In the round-about or circular, and horizontal motions of the lance, it is indispensably necessary that the lancer takes particular care never to remove the lance from his right forearm. The elbow in these motions, should always remain firmly closed upon the shaft.'

In theory, each parry was to be followed by a thrust. The cuts were parries directed against enemies on foot. If an infantry man appeared on the left and too close for a thrust to be delivered, the Lancer, according to regulations, should shorten the lance, and, at an angle of some 45 degrees:

'. . . aim a vigorous oblique stroke of the lance to the left, by carrying the spear from top to bottom, from above the horse's head, rather grazing his near shoulder, and sweeping the point round to his left, so as to parry the bayonet or give a severe cut on the head, arms or breast.'

Having thus discouraged his opponent, the Lancer should point at him. A similar movement could be performed to the right. If he had foes on foot to left and right, the Lancer could cut to his left and use the butt of the lance as a club to the right.

Not all the movements which the Lancer was trained to perform were safe or useful on service. de Brack believed that only the cuts, parries, *alentour parez* and thrusts within the front semicircle were practical in the field. He also believed that of these movements, only the forward thrusts were truly effective, but he did say that: '. . . the strokes of a lance in good order, are almost always fatal when delivered at the body.'

A claim which is not entirely acceptable. After Waterloo an officer of the Scots Greys visited Brussels and recorded that: 'I found many of our men with ten and twelve lance wounds in them, and one man, Lock, had seventeen or eighteen and lived.'

Furthermore, if fighting cuirassiers, Lancers would find attempts to attack the body futile; in October 1812 at Spass Kouplia a body of Cossacks found that their lances were shattered on impact with the plates of French cuirassiers. de Brack states that thrusts outside the prescribed area lacked vigour and precision, and could be easily parried, or the shaft of the lance could be seized by an enemy thus effectively disarming the Lancer. He remarks that movements other than thrusts could only wound; but a wound on the left arm could deny a trooper control of his horse, and a wound on the right could disarm him; in either case he would be hors de combat.

If Lancers were matched against enemy cavalry, they would probably fight men armed with sabres. Throughout the nineteenth century a great controversy raged over which weapon, lance or sabre, was inherently superior. There is no doubt that, if in the hands of a well trained man, the lance could inspire confidence in its owner, and terror in the hearts of inexperienced opponents. Proponents of the lance claimed that: ' . . . a fine expert and vigorous lancer, would . . . annihilate any three experienced dragoons or hussars . . .' Colonel de Montmorency. And at Waterloo a Lancer gave practical support to this claim by killing Sir William Ponsonby and then disposing of three Scots Greys who came back in an attempt to save him.

The superior length of the lance was also an advantage if Lancers could face an enemy head on without exposing a flank, as happened during one phase of the engagement at Genappe. But, the lance was a liability in a close mêlée, where there could be no room to wield it. de Brack stated that Lancers who were crowded by swordsmen were lost. At Carpio in September 1811, the Lancers of Berg were attacked by the 16th Light Dragoons, and one of the British officers, Lieutenant Tomkinson, observed: 'The lancers looked well and formidable before they were broken and closed by our men, and then their lances were an encumbrance.'

In the same year both the 15th and the 12th Light Dragoons conducted experiments with the lance and concluded that the sabre was a more versatile weapon. Colonel Stewart of the 12th Light Dragoons came to a reasonable conclusion when he said that: 'Good swordsmen have no reason to fear the lance if they are equally good horse men.'

This remark probably also holds good for combats conducted on open ground, rather than in the press of a mêlée, although a long weapon is always at some advantage where there is room to use it.

Ideally, if his enemy were mounted, the Lancer would use his horsemanship to present his right to his enemies left, and then point at him. If his enemy were in flight, he would probably aim to tickle his left kidney. If his enemy was coming on, he was trained to aim his point at the waist of his opponent. A point at the enemy horse would be useless, and dangerous, for the horse would carry on forwards; and the lance shaft would break and render the Lancer defenceless, or would not, in which case it would project him over his horse's rump. A thrust at the waist was often impossible; a wise opponent would lean upon his horse's neck and so protect his stomach. The Lancer would then have to aim for the head, a small, hard target, or the chest. The chest was difficult to penetrate because the ribs could turn a point, and so the Lancer had to thrust with great force to be sure of inflicting a wound. This also was perilous. At Reichenback, de Brack saw a Lancer transfix an enemy trooper, the lance passing in through his left ribs and out through the right shoulder blade; as a result the Lancer could not withdraw his spear, and as his victim fell from his horse, he was dragged from his own. A skilful swordsman, approached by a Lancer, could parry the point of the oncoming lance upwards, run in under it and either thrust at the lancer or cut vertically down at him before he could recover his balance.

If the Lancer was in retreat, and was pursued, he could use the *alentour parez* to great effect. de Brack remarked; 'The blow cannot fail to reach the man, or the head of the horse, and the weight of the weapon doubling the force of its blow, immediately knocks the man over or stops the horse short.'

The movement could also be used if surrounded by enemy fugitives. At Berry au Bac in 1814, a regiment of Polish Lancers charged and dispersed two regiments of Cossacks. A witness reported that during the pursuit: 'Major Skarzynski performed prodigies of valour. Snatching a lance from a cossack he created a void around him by knocking over the fugitives in his path . . .'

However, in retreat, a lance could also be a hindrance. At Carpio, in Spain, the Lancers were forced to fall back, and Lieutenant Tomkinson observed that their weapons: '. . . caught on the ground, caught in the appointments of other men, and pulled more dragoons off their horses than anything else.'

Against infantry, the Lancer could use points and cuts. The cuts could discourage and wound, but were rarely fatal; at Dresden in 1813 some Austrian infantry stood firm in their squares despite having fingers chopped off by Lancers. When thrusting against infantry, Lancers were almost bound to hit bone in the skull or ribs. An experienced Lancer could point precisely enough to overcome these difficulties, as an officer of the British 44th regiment at Quatre Bras observed: '. . . One of these grey-headed devils sending his lance in at the left eye of the Senior Ensign . . . down through his face until it went through his tongue and under the jaw . . .'

A less expert lancer could come to grief, as observed by an officer of the 66th Foot at Albuhera: '. . . My Ensign, Hay, was run through the lungs by a lance, which came out through his back, . . . he fell but got up again. The lancer delivered another thrust, the lance striking Hay's breast bone; down he went and the Pole rolled over in the mud beside him.'

A steady and expert infantryman could sometimes meet a Lancer on equal terms and beat him. Such an incident occurred at Waterloo, and was observed by an officer of the 69th Foot who described it as follows:

'A lancer . . . made several lunges at Dooley who was wounded in the arm, and being exasperated, . . . he sprang out of the ranks and chased the lancer . . . the latter returned at full tilt . . . Dooley faced his antagonist in the open. Everybody expected to see Dooley spitted like a hog . . . however, . . . he dexterously caught the lance on his bayonet and threw the point clear of himself, and the next moment the lancer was on the ground, pierced through the body.'

Lances were exceptionally useful in dealing with infantry who decided to run for it. It was stated in the drill regulations that in open country no fugitive on foot could escape a Lancer, the lance being able to reach over walls and through hedges to seek him out. Sometimes infantry attacked by cavalry would crouch down, obviously no protection against a lance. Russian infantry charged by cavalry sometimes lay prone until the horses had ridden over them, then stood up and fired into their rear. This technique was useless against the Lancer who could reach a prone man with ease. This facility sometimes led to grimmer things; at Albuhera and Waterloo Lancers paid particular attention to the wounded and to demoralised stragglers.

Organisation, Formation and Manoeuvre

The basic organizational unit of cavalry was the regiment. The size and internal organization of each regiment fluctuated according to circumstance. Most line regiments would have about 600 men organized in four squadrons. The regiments of the Imperial Guard were larger; in 1811 the Second Lancers of the Guard numbered 800, and in 1813 Guard Cavalry regiments were expanded from five to eight squadrons.

The basic tactical unit was the squadron. Units smaller than squadrons were not usually sent into action in regular operations. A squadron in a line Lancer regiment consisted of some 150 men, divided into two companies. Each company consisted of a Captain, Lieutenant, two Second Lieutenants, a Sergeant-Major, four Sergeants, eight Corporals, two Trumpets (for signalling orders), two Craftsmen (one a farrier, the other a *fournier* to repair equipment), and 70-80 Troopers. The company was divided into two *pelotons,* each containing between 30 and 40 troopers. The *peloton* was the basic unit of manoeuvre when on service.

Lancers were often combined in formations with other types of cavalry. In Russia in 1812, Lancers were brigaded with Hussars or *Chasseurs à Cheval*. In the same campaign, one regiment of Lancers was attached to each division of Cuirassiers; but this arrangement came to an end in 1813. In 1815, Lancers were organized into brigades, and three brigades of Lancers were present at Waterloo.

Bodies of Lancers moved and fought in two types of formation, Column and Line. In general, Column was used for movement, and Line for delivering, meeting, or threatening an attack.

In Line, a squadron of Lancers was drawn up in two ranks, with a third partial rank, the *serrefile*, of craftsmen, NCOs and subalterns, to the rear of the second rank. In close order, a horse occupied one metre of front and two of depth, and the second rank would stand one metre (half a length) behind the first, with the *serrefile* one metre to its own rear. The formation, if the squadron were of 150 men, would occupy a front of 75 metres and a depth of eleven. The commander would normally be in the centre or half a length ahead of the first rank, flanked by a trumpet. Other officers and NCOs would ride on the flanks. When the squadron was in motion, the commander steered it, the officers on the flanks ensured that the ranks did not open out or crowd in, and kept dressing, usually to the right or centre. The *serrefile* ensured that the second rank kept up and could prevent any unwounded man from turning back.

If a whole regiment was drawn up in line, in close order, there would be intervals of 15 metres between squadrons; so a regiment would take up a front of 345 metres. Sometimes the regiment might be drawn up without these intervals, in 'full lines'. This formation suffered from serious deficiencies in action; in motion it was cumbersome, difficult to keep in order and control; and the lack of intervals prevented the passage of supports forward or stragglers to the rear.

On rare occasions a regiment could be drawn up

00000000000000000000000000000000000000000000000000   00000000000000000000000000000000000000000000000000   00000000000000000000000000000000000000000000000000   00000000000000000000000000000000000000000000000000
00000000000000000000000000000000000000000000000000   00000000000000000000000000000000000000000000000000   00000000000000000000000000000000000000000000000000   00000000000000000000000000000000000000000000000000
0   0   0   0   0   0   0   0   0   0   0   0

A regiment deploying in open order. Though this was not as impressive as 'rank entire' it did give an awesome impression of strength to the enemy. The second rank was normally one or two lengths to the rear.

in 'rank entire', without a second rank, this being a device to double the strength of the troops present in the eyes of an enemy.

The drill manuals attempted to ensure that whenever a regiment formed line, whatever the circumstances, the senior squadron would be on the right, and the Colonel in the centre. If a line was to adopt open order, to increase the depth of the files,

the troopers of the second rank could rein back their horses until one or two full lengths from the first; or turn left about in fours and ride to the rear as far as desired, then go left about again; or the troopers of the first rank could simply move forward. In order to extend the front of the line, the troopers could 'passage' their horses, walking them diagonally forwards and back to achieve a sideways

A regiment in continuous column of squadrons. The scale indicates the 37.5 metre front the unit would present in this formation. The commanding officer is at the centre indicated by the flag.

```
                                              ⌐|
0000000000000000000000000000000000000000000000000000000000000000000000000000000000000000000
0000000000000000000000000000000000000000000000000000000000000000000000000000000000000000000
0                   0                   0                   0                   0
0000000000000000000000000000000000000000000000000000000000000000000000000000000000000000000
0000000000000000000000000000000000000000000000000000000000000000000000000000000000000000000
0                   0                   0                   0                   0
0000000000000000000000000000000000000000000000000000000000000000000000000000000000000000000
0000000000000000000000000000000000000000000000000000000000000000000000000000000000000000000
0                   0                   0                   0                   0
0000000000000000000000000000000000000000000000000000000000000000000000000000000000000000000
0000000000000000000000000000000000000000000000000000000000000000000000000000000000000000000
0                   0                   0                   0                   0
```

Metres

```
0              10              20              30            37.5
```

shift, sometimes towards the flanks from the centre, but usually leftwards, the right marker standing firm. If the line were in motion, the front could be extended, or closed up again until the troopers were riding boot to boot in close order, by 'inclining', inducing the horse to move diagonally.

Lancers were in column if their formation consisted of more than two full ranks. A great variety of columns were employed.

When on the march, if the route lay across open country, cavalry could move in open columns of squadrons, companies, or *pelotons*. A regiment in open column of companies, the intervals between successive companies being at 'quarter distance' (a quarter of the extent of the front of the column) from each other, would have a front of 37 metres and a depth of 127. If they were forced to march on a road, or on the beaten path beside a road, cavalry moved in column of route. A column of route normally had a front of four troopers; on a narrow or crowded way it could be reduced to two. In such a column, the front was usually extended so as to open the files and avoid jostling and galling by the horses, but the successive ranks were kept well closed up to provide room for troops coming up in the rear. A squadron in column of fours would probably be seven metres wide and about 110 metres deep. The column would consist of alternate ranks of four front rank men followed by four rear rank men. Lances were slung or held at the 'carry', held upright in the stirrup ring by the right hand. The column could change direction by wheeling or inclining.

When commencing a march, cavalry would normally walk their horses, at a speed of five kilometres per hour, for an hour, rest for ten minutes, then trot at ten kilometres per hour for two hours, then rest again. The cycle could be repeated. Sometimes an entire day's march would be done at the walk. As an additional measure to save the horses, conscientious troopers would dismount when ascending and descending hills.

When approaching the enemy, cavalry would usually adopt a broader and shallower column, probably open column of squadrons, with each squadron at quarter, half, full, or even double distance from the next. Such a column could change direction with ease if in motion, and was also able to change to another formation with rapidity. A close column, in which there might be an interval of five metres between successive squadrons, or contiguous column, in which there would be about one metre, might be formed if the battlefield were crowded and it was necessary to occupy a minimum of ground. Such a column could move forwards, but would find difficulty in changing direction or formation. It

A regiment in open column of squadrons at quarter distance. The arrow indicates how the rear ranks would deploy into column of route.

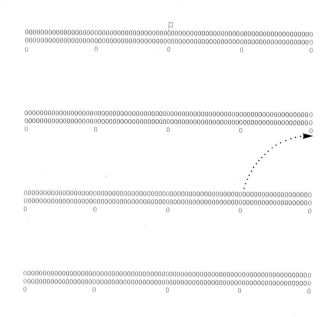

Squadrons in echelon at quarter distance, right ahead. This formation allowed successive units to form the rear and flank of the body to their front.

was also dangerous if used within sight of enemy artillery; a single cannon ball striking a close column of cavalry at 800 metres range could smash a dozen horses and injure a score more. If the regiment were in open column at full distance, with 75 metres between squadrons, a ball striking the first squadron would normally pass over the heads of the second, and so casualties and disorganisation could be minimised. So as a general rule, cavalry were put into open column or line as soon as they came within sight and artillery range of the enemy; and were closed up only when concealed or well to the rear.

Lancers also frequently adopted formations *en échelon* and *en échiquier*. *Echelon* was a staggered column, successive units in line forming to the rear and flank of the body to their front. In *échiquier,* units in line were drawn up in a chequer board pattern.

'Evolutions' comprised changes of formation, and changes of direction when in formation. Rapid and smooth changes from column to line, and vice versa, and changes of front when in line, were vital to success in action.

On the parade ground, movements from one formation to another, or from one direction when in line to another, were performed by 'fours', units of four files, to preserve dressing and to ensure that the senior squadron ended up on the right of the line or at the head of the column. These evolutions were impressive to the eye, and by using them a regiment could change formation or front using a minimum of ground. But, they were unnecessary and too complicated for use in action, where movements were usually conducted by *peloton*, with a front of some 18 men, and were much simpler.

de Brack observed that when on service, parade drills were unnecessarily complex and dangerous. He remarked that it was not necessary to save space by moving in fours as : 'On service you always have much more space than you require for your deployments.'

The parade evolutions were dangerous because they took too much time to perform. Further, the battlefield was never as clear or even as the parade square, and the troopers could never be as calm, especially if under fire. Complicated movements could easily lead to confusion and disorder, and invite an enemy attack.Many parade evolutions consisted of two distinct movements, and entailed a halt with a flank presented to the intended front at the end of the evolution, and others required the troopers to countermarch. de Brack considered that if a unit presented flanks or rear to the enemy on a battlefield, the morale, order and cohesion of the troopers must inevitably suffer. He summed up his views as follows:

'The art of manoeuvring on the field of battle consists in never being flurried, never wittingly being disadvantageously pressed by the enemy, and in profiting by every feature of the ground, and by any events which may give the superiority.'

These principles could only be applied if the units involved in a manoeuvre were able to maintain good order, and were allowed sufficient room to move with confidence. Sometimes a commander would neglect these requirements in an excess of zeal for the principle of concentration of force at the decisive point! At Wachau, in October 1813, Colonel Cathcart observed a force of some 5,000 French cavalry in an attack led by Murat: 'The French advanced, in line of contiguous columns of regiments, certainly in one body only, . . . with no sort of second line or reserve . . . The narrowness of the front to be attacked, as well as the nature of the ground, caused this powerful force to crowd together in one dense mass . . . '

In consequence, forward movement was halted by a shallow ditch to the front. Whilst the French were halted, a brigade of Cossacks (perhaps 2,000 strong) appeared on one flank. The French were unable to move rapidly to flank or rear, and panicked. Thus, 2,000 Cossacks routed a mixed French cavalry force of 5,000. Ney perpetrated a similar blunder at Waterloo, where he ordered an attack by forty squadrons on a front wide enough for eight. The squadrons suffered heavily from the British artillery in their dense formation, and crowded together for moral support. A British officer observed: 'Their ranks were so closely pressed that the horses were actually lifted off the ground by the pressure.'

A prudent cavalry commander would allow his troops plenty of elbow-room, especially if they were in motion, and keep the movements simple.

As a column of route in fours approached the likely area of engagement, it would normally go into open column of squadrons. If this formation were to be based on the leading squadron, the front four files would by inclining or wheeling reach the right of the desired front for the new formation, and halt. The successive fours would then incline left and come up to halt on the left, until the whole squadron was in line. The next squadron would form in the same manner to the rear of the first. When all the squadrons were so formed in line, the regiment could move off. Really experienced troops could perform this evolution on the move.

If an open column of squadrons was to form line, the leading squadron would take ground on the right of the desired new front, and the others incline or wheel to the left, come up level with the first, and halt at a suitable interval away. If the senior squadron was not at the head of the column, and the commander demanded his proper place, the leading squadron would halt at the centre of the new front, and the rest of the squadrons come up *en evantail* by inclining to right and left in turn. If it were desired to form line to the flank or rear of a column, the column would normally wheel until it faced the new direction, and then form line in the usual way. A column required to form line in the rear of its current position could wheel round about, go to the rear as far as necessary, wheel about again, and form line. When performing such expansive movements, cavalry preferred to wheel to the right. Often, such movements would be done by successive *pelotons*, smaller units being easier to keep closed up when wheeling. By a combination of wheeling and inclining, it was possible to base a line on virtually any squadron in an open column, and to face the line in any direction.

A regiment had even more flexibility, and considerably more speed, in its evolutions, if it were in open column at full distance. In this formation, it could form line to the right simply by wheeling all squadrons to the right. A regiment at quarter distance approached on the flank by an enemy would often go to full distance by moving squadrons forward, and then wheel them to the right in this manner. A regiment in open column at full distance would normally face to the rear by wheeling right about by *pelotons*. Open column at full distance was often used as an attacking formation. At Waterloo, Jacquinot's Lancer brigade moved up in open column of squadrons at full distance to attack the spent British heavy cavalry. At Quatre Bras, Lancers moved up in open columns at double distance, there being 150 metres between squadrons.

Echelon was also a flexible and advantageous formation used for movement and in attack. From open *échelon*, a regiment could form line or any sort of column with ease, simply by the squadrons going forward and inclining. *Echelon* could change front very swiftly, if a regiment were in *échelon* of squadrons at full distance, with the right squadron ahead, it could meet a threat on the left flank by wheeling all squadrons to the left, so going into *échelon* left ahead. The formation also allowed the commanders of each squadron a better view to the front and flanks than an ordinary column. Regiments in line often placed a single *peloton* in *échelon* in order to secure a flank, and if a regiment of four squadrons was in *échelon*, squadrons one, two and three would each have their rear and one flank secured. *Echelon* also confused enemy artillery; from a few hundred metres it was easily taken for line. A regiment in *échelon* had most of the advantages of line without the disadvantages; the whole strength of the regiment was deployed facing the enemy, and it was easier to keep good order and dressing. *Echelon* was a useful formation when crossing a country with enclosures, as it could by the squadrons inclining rapidly extend or contract its front. *Echelon* could be formed, on a large scale, from units in line or in column. During Ney's grand cavalry assault at Waterloo, Lancers moved up in squadron columns, echeloned to the left rear of the great mass of Cuirassiers. On the extreme left of the French line of battle, Colonel Thackwell of the 15th Light Dragoons observed a brigade of Lancers advancing:- '. . . I distinctly saw the three lines of the enemy's cavalry advancing, rather en échelon . . .'

The Lancers were then observed by Major Mercer of the R.H.A. to form in 'full lines' (and were possibly also in 'line entire'.) Their intention was evidently to draw some British cavalry away from the decisive point of action by moving on the flank. In this they succeeded for a while, as Sir Colquhoun Grant's brigade was sent to watch them.

Echiquier was a useful formation for covering a retreat; squadrons could alternately retire and support, and so fall back with a sense of security. If very close to an enemy, or about to deliver or receive a charge, lancers might manoeuvre in line, changing front by wheeling the whole regiment, or, if there

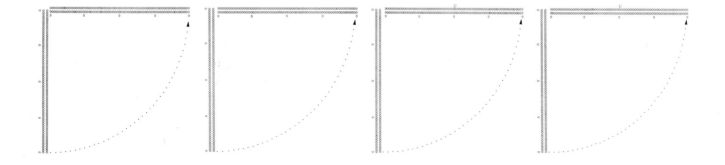

A regiment deploying from open column at full distance into line. This formation was easy to adopt since squadrons simply wheeled right to deploy.

was not room for such an extensive movement, wheeling by squadrons or *pelotons*. When moving in line, the first rank would have lances at 'Guard', the second rank would keep their lance points on a level with the caps of the first rank, or sling lances and draw their sabres. If the front narrowed, a line could form into column in various ways. If the column were to be formed to the front, the squadron or *peloton* on the right would go forward, and the next on the left go forward and incline right until it covered the rear of the first. The other units would follow on in the same way. If the column were to be formed to a flank, the squadrons or *pelotons* would simply wheel until they faced in the new direction, then move off.

A regiment suddenly threatened by attack on all sides could protect itself by forming square. To form square it had first to form open column of squadrons at full distance. Then, the two middle squadrons wheeled their left flank companies to the left, and their right flank companies to the right. The rear squadron would advance, then wheel about by fours. The front ranks of the square held their lances at a low 'Guard' position, whilst the second ranks prepared carbines or pistols. If the time required to form square was lacking, a regiment could form close column of squadrons. Then, the front rank would lower lances to 'Guard', the left and right flank files point to left and right respectively, and the rear rank reverse lances. This formation was used in Russia by the Poles, and was extremely successful against the Cossacks.

Sometimes Lancers would move in a kind of open order which had no apparent formation at all, a manoeuvre they probably learnt from the Cossacks. In Spring 1814 Napoleon raised a force of 1,200

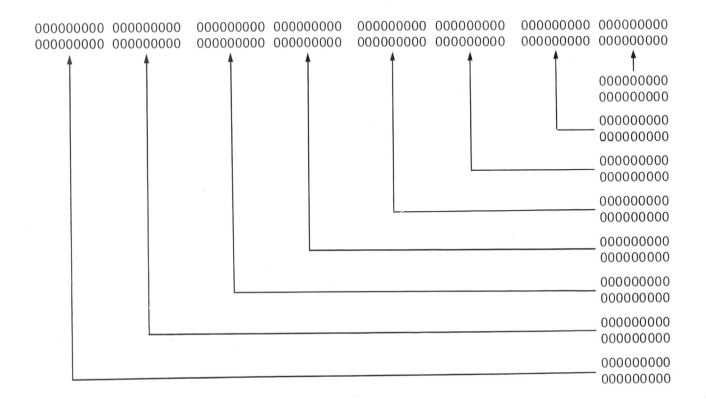

A regiment deploying from close column of companies to line to the front.

Poles at Paris, and wrote to his brother Joseph that they were to be his Cossacks. At Quatre Bras an officer of the 44th observed Lancers bearing down on skirmishers, stragglers and wounded near the British squares 'like a swarm of bees'. During the battle of Waterloo an officer of the Inniskilling Dragoons remarked that Lancers attacked the disorganized and blown troopers of the Union Brigade in 'clouds'. This nebulous sort of formation had obvious advantages when crossing bad ground, pursuing dispersed enemies, or attempting to reduce the effects of enemy fire power.

On the parade ground, evolutions and manoeuvres could be conducted at the gallop, at a speed of some 300 metres per minute. On service they would be done at the trot (240 metres per minute) or the walk (100 metres per minute).

Some commanders seem to have regarded

Deploying from echelon of squadrons right ahead at full distance to left ahead at half distance.

evolutions and manoeuvres as ends in themselves, and practiced them relentlessly in search of choreographic perfection. In battle, they were simply means of taking advantageous ground, or preparing to charge with effect.

Within the line of battle, light cavalry would normally be posted in line or open column on the flanks of the front line, to guard the flanks and be ready to cover a retreat or pursue after a victory. If in second line or reserve, they would often be placed in rear of the centre of the front line, ready to reinforce either flank. Here they would usually be beyond the sight and artillery range of the enemy, and would usually stand in close column; ready to move and conserving space.

A great deal of manoeuvring was directed to the seizure of a good position. A good position for cavalry had certain clear characteristics; flanks secured by friendly troops or by the terrain; a secure route to the rear; and a clear view of ground to the front were all great advantages. High ground was of great value; it afforded a good view, concealment from the enemy and protection from his fire, and it forced the enemy to climb if he attacked. If the position were a defensive one, an obstacle to the front was an advantage, as it would check and disorganise an enemy advance. On the left flank of the French army at Waterloo, the Lancers sent to threaten but not actually attack the British extreme right, took post in line behind a ravine.

A position with a defile to the rear was bad, the defile would obstruct a retreat, and this knowledge would upset the troopers. A position with one flank protected by bad ground or a natural obstacle, and the other open, was also bad; an attack on the open flank could drive its victims into the bad ground, or pin them against the obstacle.

Lancers in Battle

In battle Lancers performed various duties, some defensive, some offensive, some the traditional preserve of light cavalry, and some supposedly reserved for heavy cavalry.

Light cavalry were employed to protect the flanks and rear of the main line of battle, and to threaten the flanks and rear of the enemy lines. At Waterloo one brigade of Lancers was sent to the right flank of the French army to watch out for the approach of the Prussians. Another was sent to the left flank to feint at the right of the Allied forces, and distract some British Light Cavalry.

Light cavalry were sent forward to discover the size, position, deployment and movements of enemy forces, and to conceal the state of friendly forces from the enemy. This entailed the destruction, subjugation or containment of the enemy light troops sent forward into no man's land. This work was done by skirmishing.

In a defensive battle, cavalry of all sorts would be used as a mobile reserve, to provide swift reinforcement to any part of the line of battle under severe pressure, and to charge any enemy force that penetrated it. It could also help to hold a position by standing some 70 metres behind the line to be maintained, and charging any enemy unit which crossed it. By such means it could defend the flanks of infantry and artillery. After such a charge, if the protected unit was infantry, the cavalry, if successful, would pursue the enemy a few hundred metres, then return to its post. If the protected unit was a battery, the cavalry would not pursue, but retire swiftly and allow the guns to pour grapeshot into the checked or fleeing enemy. When unsuccessful in such a charge, the cavalry would fall back behind its infantry or artillery, and rely upon them to hold the enemy with their fire until it had re-formed and prepared itself to charge again. Such cavalry would normally stand to the rear and to a flank of the unit it protected, in order to have room to charge and to avoid fire directed against the _protégé_. It would be concealed if possible, to give it the advantage of surprise in an attack.

If the line of battle was forced to fall back, the light cavalry would cover the retirement, and provide a rear guard. They would attempt to hold off the enemy by charging at opportunity, holding defiles, conducting ambushes, and hovering on the heads and flanks of pursuing columns. After Waterloo, Piré's Lancer brigade covered the retreat of the remnants of the French army.

In an offensive action, lancers would cooperate with infantry and artillery to destroy the enemy line of battle.

Firstly, by skirmishing and charging they would discover the enemy forces and drive in the enemy light cavalry. Next, they would by threatening or actually charging, force the enemy infantry to form square, as they did at Quatre Bras and at Waterloo. Whilst they hovered within charging distance of the squares, the enemy infantry in them could be subjected to a most destructive bombardment. Sometimes horse artillery came up close enough to fire grape or canister into the squares; at Waterloo some English squares were fired on from a range of 60 metres by French horse guns. Meanwhile infantry columns of attack would come up to assault the enemy, and to prepare the way for them, light cavalry could clear the enemy light infantry. Once the combined effects of bombardment and musketry or bayonet attack had reduced, shaken and disordered the enemy infantry, cavalry could charge to complete their ruin. Cavalry could sometimes be sent round the enemy flank to attack his infantry in flank and rear whilst friendly infantry engaged it to the front; this was done at Albuhera with great success.

When the enemy began to retreat, it was the task of the light cavalry to pursue, and to turn retreat into rout. The best way to do this was to evade the enemy rearguard, march parallel to the retreating enemy column, and attack its flanks. This type of action was difficult to carry out, but would ensure dispersal and demoralisation of the enemy forces without the casualties entailed by attacks on a well controlled enemy rear guard.

Cavalry could never act in a defensive way, even when forced to retreat, survival depended upon the ability to suddenly turn and charge the pursuing enemy. Cavalry could hold ground by skirmishing, but only if the enemy concerned was content to limit his own action to skirmishing. If the enemy moved forward a formed body, of infantry or cavalry, cavalry could only charge or retreat.

However, skirmishing usually preceded and followed every major clash of arms. The objects of skirmishing were to discover the nature of the ground ahead, to find and annoy enemy forces, and prevent similar activity by enemy light troops.

If ordered to skirmish a Lancer regiment would send forward the left and right flank *pelotons* of each squadron, which would amount to half of its total strength. Once in sight of the enemy, the *pelotons* would halt. Half would remain in position, formed

up in line, with lances at the 'guard'. The other *pelotons* would go forward 100 to 150 metres, lances slung over the left shoulder, carbines and pistols prepared, and by inclining as they advanced go into skirmish formation. In this formation individual troopers were formed into three vague ranks, with distances of 10 – 30 metres between ranks and intervals of about 10 – 15 metres between files. The files were staggered, so that the whole formation was a sort of loose *échiquier*.

The formation was supposed to extend beyond the flanks of the regiment, and of the enemy force to the front.

Once they were in position, having occupied any high ground available and taken advantage of cover, skirmishers commenced firing and retiring by ranks. Each front rank trooper would, whilst constantly riding to and fro to disturb the enemy's aim, find a mark to his left, and fire at it, taking care not to burn or alarm his horse whilst doing so. His second rank coverer would then come up, and when he was two-thirds of the way to the front rank, the front rank trooper turned away to his right, and rode back into the rear rank, where he reloaded his carbine. The new front rank man would not fire until his new rear rank coverer was fully prepared to fire. By this process skirmishers were supposed to keep up a regular fire upon the enemy.

If an enemy mounted skirmisher came forward to charge, the lancer would put his carbine in the holster, take his sabre in his right hand to meet his opponent's first cut or thrust, and hold his pistol in his left hand to use at opportunity.

If the enemy sent forward a formed body, the skirmishers could fall back on their immediate supports, the formed *pelotons*, and form into line. If further pressed, these troops could fall back on the rest of the regiment.

When advancing or falling back, to conform to movements by the regiment, skirmishers would carry on the usual system of firing and moving by turns, but when advancing the front rank would stand firm having fired, and the second and third ranks would 'leapfrog' through. When in retreat the front rank would fire and retire to the rear, the second rank would not move up, but stand firm and prepare to fire.

Cavalry skirmishers were most effective in open country, and in such terrain could make the work of enemy light infantry impossible. At Quatre Bras the British 44th Foot sent out two companies to skirmish. They were swiftly surrounded by Lancers and cut off from their regiment. In order to escape annihilation they formed a line four deep and charged with the bayonet back to their regiment.

At Genappe the French combined Lancers and light infantry in a skirmishing force that was able to harass the 7th Hussars with impunity, as observed by Captain William Verner of that regiment: '. . . the enemy's skirmishers were coming forward, each man having a sharpshooter on the horse behind him, who got off, took deliberate aim, and when he was pursued, jumped upon the horse, cantered away . . .'

Skirmishers were often sent forward to prepare for a charge. They did this by surveying the ground over which the charge was to be made. Sometimes they would try to prepare the enemy force for attack by pressing back its own skirmishers, and by firing upon it, to disorder it. But most skirmishing had no positive results at all, and whole days were whiled away in desultory expenditure of powder and shot.

The most important form of cavalry action in battle was the charge. Correct timing, superior morale, suitable formation, firm discipline and order, a good pace, proper armament and skilful use of supports were essential to a successful charge. The achievement of surprise, or an attack on the enemy flanks or rear would greatly increase the chances of success.

Cavalry rarely charged an enemy in good order with success. Charges were normally delivered when the enemy had been reduced, shaken and disordered by artillery and infantry. At Quatre Bras and Waterloo French cavalry attacked squares of British infantry that had been reduced by bombardment, and in the case of Waterloo, by infantry attack as well; but they had not been disordered or demoralised, so the charges failed.

Cavalry sent to charge the enemy were usually organized into three distinct elements; the assault force, the supports, and the reserve. Each of these elements had a distinct *rôle* to play during each of the five phases into which a charge can be divided.

During the *approach* to the enemy, all three elements would probably move as one body, in close column of squadrons. This formation allowed the commander to move his force rapidly in any direction under immediate control, and would conceal the strength of the force.

Just before coming into effective range of the enemy, the rearmost squadrons, destined to act as the reserve, would halt. If possible, they would take post behind cover. They would remain formed up in close column, ready to move. The squadrons of the assault force and the supports would continue forward, going into open order to reduce the effects of enemy fire, to enter the phase of the *advance*. During the advance the assault force would probably form into Line or *échelon*, being careful to maintain intervals between the squadrons so that the wounded could go to the rear without impeding their progress, the supports could come forward if necessary, and good order could be maintained. The supports would keep station some 60 metres behind, so that if the assault force were checked they would not run into them, but could still support them rapidly if necessary. Supports would normally be formed in Line, open columns or *échelon* at this stage. As the assault force squadrons came closer to

Trooper in full dress,
elite company,
7th Polish Light Horse
Lancers, 1811-1813.

Trooper in full dress,
centre company,
7th Polish Light Horse
Lancers, 1811-1815.

Trumpeter in full dress,
elite company,
7th Polish Light Horse
Lancers, 1813-1814.

Trooper in campaign
dress, 1st Regiment of
the Lancers of the
Vistula, 1808-1811.

Trooper in service dress,
elite company,
8th Polish Light Horse
Lancers, 1811-1813.

Trumpeter in campaign
dress, centre company,
7th Polish Light Horse
Lancers, 1813.

Trumpeter in full dress,
elite company,
8th Polish Light Horse
Lancers, 1811-1813.

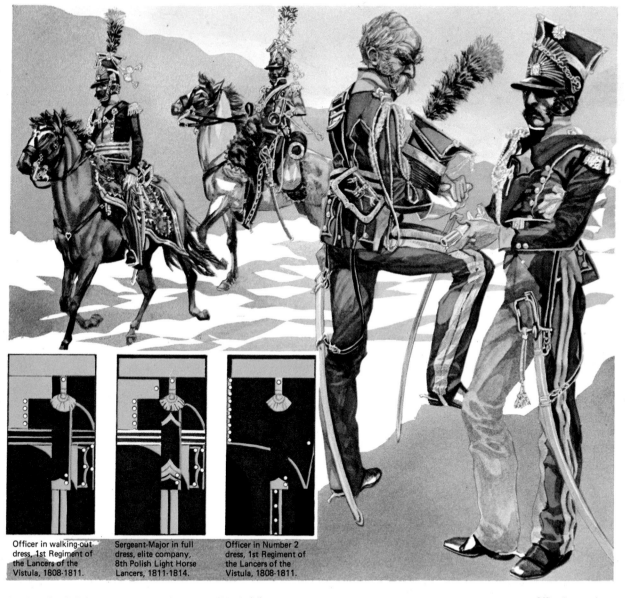

Officer in walking-out
dress, 1st Regiment of
the Lancers of the
Vistula, 1808-1811.

Sergeant-Major in full
dress, elite company,
8th Polish Light Horse
Lancers, 1811-1814.

Officer in Number 2
dress, 1st Regiment of
the Lancers of the
Vistula, 1808-1811.

Superior officer in full
dress, 1st Regiment of
the Lancers of the
Vistula, 1809.

Trumpet-Major in full
dress, 1st Regiment of
the Lancers of the
Vistula, 1809.

Officer in full dress,
7th Polish Light Horse
Lancers, 1811-1814.

Officer in campaign
dress, 7th Polish
Light Horse Lancers,
1811-1814.

the enemy, they steadily increased their speed. At this stage the outcome of the attack could be decided by the relative morale of the forces involved. The assault force might lose heart, come to a halt some distance from the enemy, and stand in hesitation, or attempt to retreat, in which case it would be vulnerable to counter-attack, especially if the enemy were cavalry; or it might decide not to charge home too late to halt, and wheel as a body, collection of small bodies, or confused mass, to left or right or both, round the flanks of the enemy unit. On the other hand, the enemy might be demoralised by the rapid advance of the cavalry; enemy cavalry might retreat rather than stand or counter-charge; enemy infantry might surrender, or attempt to run, or panic and lose formation. If the enemy fled from the cavalry, the advance would become a pursuit, normally part of the fifth phase of a charge. But, if the cavalry continued to move forward and the enemy met them, the charge would enter the *impact* phase as the two forces collided.

The aim of the assault force during the *impact* phase was to use the shock of collision to demoralise and disorder the enemy and themselves retain sufficient order and control to exploit the momentary confusion of the enemy. This required them to combine order with speed, of which all authorities agreed that order was of the greater importance. The drill book stated that: 'A well directed charge of cavalry should be solid, silent, and steady, like a moving wall of men and horses, advancing to the attack in regular and compact order.'

Weight gave more impetus than speed, and if the horses were spurred to a gallop too early, they would not only disorder the ranks, but arrive at the enemy line weak and blown. Usually, cavalry would trot to within 60 metres or so of the enemy (if they could be held under control for long enough), and would then start to gallop. At the same time they would lower their weapons, point towards the enemy, shout, and lean forward on their horses' necks for protection. Meanwhile the supports would trot up to within 60 metres of the enemy, and halt or continue on, according to the fortunes of the assault force. When the assault force hit the enemy, the task of the front rank was to break through his first line of men and disorder him, the second rank, half a length behind, replaced those in the front rank who fell, and tried to force their way into the enemy formation. Lancers were at an advantage in the advance and impact phases of a charge because of the reputation and length of their weapons. Because their weapons were long and conferred such an advantage when charging in good order in line, enemy troops, especially if they were raw were sometimes frightened by the appearance of lancers into flight or surrender. During the impact, lancers could reach men with swords or bayonets who could not reach them. In order to capitalise on the advantages of the lance, which depended upon the maintenance of good dressing in the line, Lancers usually did not gallop against an enemy who was steady. Baron Jomini remarked that no cavalry could succeed where Cuirassiers or Lancers failed to penetrate, but that – '. . . if the cavalry is armed with the lance, the fast trot is the proper gait, since the advantageous use of that weapon depends upon the preservation of good order . . .'

The *impact* phase of a charge could result in one of three outcomes. The assault force might destroy the order and morale of the enemy force, and force it to surrender or retreat. If the enemy retreated, the supports would normally come forward whilst the assault force reorganized, and take up the position and duties of the reserve, the original reserve coming up to act as supports. The efforts of the assault force might have less adverse effects upon the enemy morale and order than on its own, and it might be repulsed in confusion. In this case it would fall back to re-form behind the supports, who would either stand and menace the enemy or swiftly subject them to a second impact, whilst the reserve advanced to act as supports. The *impact* would usually result in a *mêlée*, in which both sides would lose formation, and the soldiers would mingle in a formless mass of individual combats. The commander of each unit involved would usually attempt to keep a nucleus of men formed round himself, and preserve as much order as possible, for the most orderly force usually won a *mêlée*. But, it was almost impossible to control cavalrymen who had just sustained and survived an impact and were fighting at close quarters for life, loot and glory. If it were possible, once a *mêlée* had developed, a commander would use part of the supports or reserve to charge the rear or a flank of the enemy; in cavalry combats on a large scale victory always went to the side which preserved a formed body of troops longest in search of such an opportunity.

Lancers were at a distinct disadvantage in the *mêlée*, because there was not room to use their weapons. The lance could break open an enemy formation at impact and produce a *mêlée*; in the *mêlée* it was a liability. Jomini stated: 'The lance is the best arm for offensive purposes when a body of horsemen charge in line, for it enables them to strike an enemy who cannot reach them; but it is a very good plan to have a second rank or a reserve armed with sabres, which are more easily handled than the lance in hand to hand fighting when the ranks become broken.'

Jomini's advice was usually taken by Lancers. Before 1813 the second rank of the assault force would sling their lances and use their sabres in a charge; after 1813 they did not carry lances. The front rank would break up and penetrate the enemy line, ride beyond it, sling or discard their lances, draw sabres, and return to the fray. Meanwhile the second rank would be in amongst the enemy, hacking and hewing.

The *mêlée* could end in a mutual withdrawal of attacking and defending forces, a repulse for the attackers, or retreat for the defenders. This constituted the *aftermath* of the charge. If the result were a draw, the attacking forces could renew the assault with the supports whilst the original assault force retired, or could draw away and retreat under the protection of the threat posed by the supports, or of skirmishes provided by them. If the assault force were repulsed, the same conditions would apply, although a repulse usually had an adverse effect on morale. If the enemy fled, he could be pursued. In the pursuit the supports and reserve would move up through the disordered and tired assault force. The squadrons of the supports would send forward their flank *pelotons* (in all, half their strength), to chase and attack the enemy in open order. The centre *pelotons* remained formed up, ready to charge and disperse the enemy should any of them attempt to rally and re-form. If the enemy had a second line in the field, the cavalry would attempt to drive the fugitives into it to create confusion and panic, and if they succeeded, take advantage of the opportunity to launch another charge. Lancers had advantages when in pursuit; they could reach men lying prone and beyond hedges or other obstacles. Commanders had to take care that in the excitement of a pursuit their men did not get out of hand and gallop too far ahead to be easy prey for any formed body of enemy cavalry in the vicinity. Cavalry were at their most vulnerable just after they had delivered an assault, successful or not, for they would then be confused, disordered, reduced in numbers, and tired. The most important function of the supports and reserve was to protect the flanks and rear of the assault force from enemy horsemen, and to provide shelter for them to rally.

It seems that the key to success in cavalry action was high morale and good discipline. Only troops with good morale would vigorously gallop into

The 30th Light Horse & 9th (Polish) Light Horse Lancers of the Line

Trooper in full dress,
centre company,
30th Light Horse, 1811.

Trumpeter in full dress,
elite company, 30th
Light Horse, 1811-1812.

Corporal in full dress,
centre company,
9th Polish Light Horse
Lancers, 1812-1813.

Trooper in service dress,
centre company, 30th
Light Horse, 1811-1812.

Trooper of centre
company, 9th Polish
Light Horse Lancers,
transition period, 1812.

Trumpeter in service
dress, elite company,
9th Polish Light Horse
Lancers, transition
period, 1812.

Sergeant in campaign
dress, centre company,
9th Polish Light Horse
Lancers, 1813-1814.

Officer in full dress,
9th Polish Light Horse,
1813-1814.

Sergeant-Major in full
dress, elite company,
9th Polish Light Horse
Lancers, 1813-1814.

Officer in Number 2
dress, 9th Polish
Light Horse Lancers,
1813-1814.

Officer in campaign
dress and greatcoat,
9th Polish Light Horse
Lancers, 1813-1814.

Officer in Number 2
dress, 9th Polish
Light Horse Lancers,
1813-1814.

Officer in Number 2
dress, 30th Light Horse,
1811-1812.

Officer in campaign
dress, 30th Light Horse,
1811.

collision with enemy forces; only troops with good discipline could restrain their horses' speed and maintain the degree of order necessary to overthrow the enemy. The timing of the charge, preparation of the enemy, formation adopted and weapons used were all intended to preserve order and morale. Napoleon believed that discipline, order, speed, surprise and the use of supports to give the assault force a sense of security were the main ingredients of a successful cavalry charge. Discipline and order were the results of training and experience, but morale was much more volatile. Cavalry would, if possible, be kept under cover, away from the upsetting effects of enemy artillery, until the opportune moment for an attack arrived. At this point one could bolster morale by giving each trooper a dram. Some commanders adopted more extreme measures; de Brack stated:

'. . . if they are to charge infantry or artillery, it does no harm and gives the men nerve to expose themselves for some moments to the fire of skirmishers and to shot. Troops which have suffered losses will charge with more vigour than those which have not. Not only does suffering inspire the desire for revenge, but it is then easy to persuade the men that charging is often less dangerous than standing in position.'

Charges were usually made in Line or *échelon*. Sometimes the line could be so deployed that it struck the enemy at an oblique angle, in which case it was said to be '*en écharpe*'. This form of attack was difficult to achieve and of doubtful real advantage. *Échelon* was a most popular formation for attack, and Napoleon believed that charging cavalry were best deployed in four or five *échelons*. The first *échelon* could then act as the assault force, and the successive ones could act as supports or reserve, whilst protecting flanks and rear of elements ahead, or could deliver supplementary assaults to the enemy flanks with great expedition. It was widely believed that ten men in a flank attack were worth a hundred in a frontal attack. Cavalry would sometimes charge in open column if their front was constricted or if the troops or horses were raw and required the moral support and compulsion of troops coming up behind to induce them to ride forward against the enemy. In such a formation squadrons could be impeded and disordered by casualties or deserters from the units ahead.

The state of the ground was important. If cavalry had to charge uphill or over soft ground, their speed would be reduced, and their horses would have less vigour in impact, *mêlée* and pursuit. Cavalry which had to negotiate obstacles on their approach and advance would also go slowly, or suffer a loss of order. Hard, even, flat ground was best for cavalry charges; but cavalry made good use of hills, woods, villages and other sources of cover to obtain tactical surprise. Sometimes cavalry might be constrained by the ground to charge on a narrow front, for example, if they were on a road. In such a case the assault force would charge in column on a front as wide as the road allowed, by *pelotons*. Of the leading squadron, the first *peloton* would be in column some 30 metres ahead of the second; the third and fourth being drawn up together some 30 metres further to the rear. The second, third and fourth *pelotons* would act as supports, and would deploy their front across half the width of the road, to provide an escape for the charging *peloton* if it suffered a repulse. The second squadron would be drawn up across half the road some 70 metres to the rear of the first. In a sustained action, the *pelotons*, and then the squadrons, could be isolated, so as always to have fresh troops in an assault.

It was best to attack the enemy cavalry when they were in line and had exposed a flank, were moving or changing formation, blown after a charge, or disordered by fire. French cavalry often used fire or manoeuvre to disrupt an enemy cavalry formation prior to a charge. In 1814 at Hoogstaaten a mixed force of Lancers and Carabiniers faced some Prussian Uhlans. The Carabiniers fired a volley into the Prussians to disrupt them, and the subsequent charge was a complete success. Sometimes cavalry were supported by horse artillery which broke up the enemy before a charge. Cavalry sometimes masked horse guns and annoyed enemy cavalry so as to draw them into ambush. At Romanovo in the Ukraine, in July 1812, Ataman Platov of the Don Cossacks formed his squadrons in line before a bridge. A Polish Lancer brigade led by Tyskiewicz came up and charged. Platov's force counter-charged, forced back Tyskiewicz and fell back. Another Lancer brigade advanced led by Rozniecki, and pursued the Cossacks, whereupon the Russians drew aside to expose the unfortunate Poles to the fire of hidden guns and infantry.

The enemy could sometimes be tricked into giving up a good position or disturbing his formation by sending a squadron in column of *pelotons* off towards his flank. As the enemy attempted to adjust his deployment to meet the new threat, he could be charged from the front.

Simple frontal assaults on cavalry were rarely decisive. French cavalry were accustomed to charge front and flank simultaneously. For this reason, *échelon* was a most popular formation. If an attacking force were in four *échelons*, the first could shake the enemy by frontal shock, the second take a flank, and the third and fourth act as supports and reserve.

Supports were vital to security in a cavalry action, as only they could save the assault force from a cavalry counter-attack when it was at its most vulnerable, just after a charge. Jomini stated that in a cavalry action: '. . . the victory will remain with the party having the last squadrons in reserve in readiness to be thrown upon the flank of the enemy's line while his front is engaged.'

At Wachau a force of Polish Lancers and Dragoons of the Imperial Guard attacked three regiments of Russian Cuirassiers in front and flank, and drove them off. They themselves were then defeated by some more Cuirassiers who attacked the front of the dragoons and the flanks of the Lancers.

During the nineteenth century a great controversy raged over the merits of various types of cavalry. Some claimed that light cavalry could not attack heavy. French Lancers frequently attacked Cuirassiers. The recommended methods were to torment the heavies to tire them and provoke them to charge. When they did Lancers might wheel outwards from the centre at a late stage in their advance, and as the heavies rode through the gap, wheel round their flanks and charge them in the rear. A more bloody method was to form up in column of squadrons or companies, counter-charge and break through the centre of the heavies' line, then wheel to take them in the rear.

It was also claimed that other types of cavalry could not overcome Lancers. This was not so. At Genappe the Lifeguards charged and routed the French Lancers who had just repelled three charges by the 7th Hussars. At Waterloo Jacquinot's Lancer brigade was attacked 'en écharpe' in front by the 16th Light Dragoons and simultaneously on the right flank by the 12th Light Dragoons, and thrown back. At Espeja in September 1811, three squadrons of the 14th Light Dragoons made a frontal attack upon a French force of four squadrons, two of them Lancers, two *Chasseurs à* Chèval. The Light Dragoons broke through the Lancers' formation and sabred them, and they fell back.

However, there is no doubt that if arranged in line, in good order, with flanks secured, Lancers were at advantage in receiving an attack. In 1812 at Maloyaroslavetz two squadrons of Lancers were suddenly attacked by a loose formation of some 2,000 Cossacks. They formed close column and

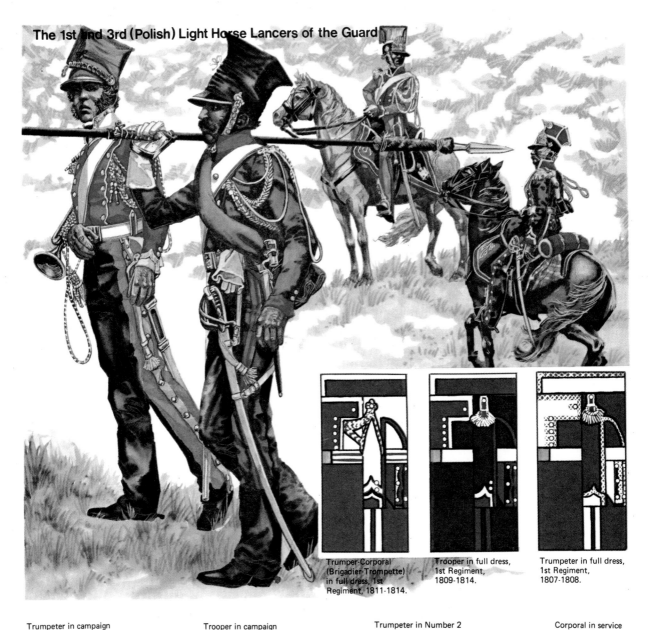

The 1st and 3rd (Polish) Light Horse Lancers of the Guard

Trumper-Corporal
(Brigadier-Trompette)
in full dress, 1st
Regiment, 1811-1814.

Trooper in full dress,
1st Regiment, 1809-1814.

Trumpeter in full dress,
1st Regiment, 1807-1808.

Trumpeter in campaign
dress, 3rd Regiment,
1812.

Trooper in campaign
dress, 1st Regiment,
1813.

Trumpeter in Number 2
dress, 1st Regiment,
1810-1814.

Corporal in service
dress, 1st Regiment,
1807-1809

Trumpet-Major in
campaign dress, 1st
Regiment, 1809-1814.

Master-Farrier (Maitre-
Ouvrier) in full dress,
1st Regiment, 1809.

Officer in ball dress,
1st Regiment, 1810.

Regimental Sergeant-
Major (Marechal-des-
logis-chef) in full
dress, 1st Regiment,
1807-1809.

Trumpet-Major in full
dress, 1st Regiment,
1809-1814.

Superior officer in full
dress, 3rd Regiment,
1812-1813.

Officer in Campaign
dress, 1st Regiment,
1809-1814.

presented their lances, and the Cossacks held back. de Brack claims that at Waterloo the British Cavalry avoided making frontal attacks on Lancers.

Cavalry threatened with a charge could take various measures to defend themselves. If possible, they would take position behind an obstacle, and counter-charge when the enemy was confused by it. They could draw back or provoke the enemy, so that he might gallop too soon and arrive with blown horses and supports too far in the rear. If the enemy charged from the correct distance, it was best to launch a counter-charge when he was a quarter of the way along his route; in that way the defending unit could achieve almost the same speed as the attacker, and usually keep better order. Sometimes French cavalry delivered a volley from their carbines before making a counter-charge. This procedure was of doubtful value; if they fired soon enough to enable them to charge properly, the enemy would be beyond effective range, and would be encouraged by the failure of the volley to take effect; if the volley were given at effective range, there would be no time to reach effective speed in the counter-charge. Sometimes Lancers stood still and relied on the length of their weapons to deter the enemy and protect them.

Lancers fought their most effective action against cavalry at Waterloo. The British Household and Union Brigades delivered a great charge against the French infantry columns of attack, got out of hand, and galloped across heavy ground into the French artillery lines, where they arrived without supports or reserves and in disorder. Jacquinot's Lancer brigade came up, charged their flanks and rear in open column, and did great execution. Colonel de Lacy Evans observed: '. . . The French Lancers continued to advance on our left in good order. If we could have formed a hundred men we could have made a respectable retreat and saved many; but we could effect no formation, and were helpless . . . it was in this part of the transaction almost the whole of the loss of the Brigade took place.

Cavalry used different techniques when charging infantry. Infantry could not counter-charge or pursue repulsed cavalry, but they could stop a charge by fire. It was best to charge infantry when they were in line or open column, especially if they were on the move, or if they could be approached from flanks or rear. Cavalry could not attack the front of a steady line of infantry, or infantry in close column or square with any prospect of success, unless the enemy could be shaken by artillery support, or were unable to deliver effective fire.

Cavalry could attempt to overcome the infantry fire in various ways. They would attack a line of infantry *en écharpe*, because oblique fire was less effective than direct fire. If faced by a square, cavalry could try to induce the infantry to fire too soon, and spur on to a full gallop once the first volley had been given to reach the enemy before they could reload. When attacking line or square cavalry often charged in successive lines. The first line would draw the enemy fire, suffer a repulse, and wheel away, whilst the second rode into the infantry. Often, two squadrons would attack two faces of a square simultaneously to draw their fire, and a third squadron would then attack the corner where those faces met.

Lancers were supposed to be particularly effective against infantry, especially infantry who could not fire. It was believed that the length of their weapons gave them a critical advantage, and that infantry faced by Lancers would be demoralised by the sight of them. This reputation was built upon spectacular successes at Albuhera, Dresden and Katzbach, it can be undermined by failures in other actions.

At Quatre Bras and Waterloo Lancers never broke into a single well-formed square of steady infantry despite massive artillery support. At both these battles the importance of morale was illustrated. At Quatre Bras Piré's Lancers destroyed a battalion square of raw Hanoverian *landwehr* without any support from guns. In contrast, British battalions in square at Quatre Bras and Waterloo sustained immense casualties from the French bombardments yet were not broken. Their steadiness intimidated the French cavalry. At Quatre Bras Lancers charged up to squares in good order, to be repulsed by volleys at about 15 metres range. These volleys would destroy the front rank, whose bodies would impede the second rank. The French attacks were badly co-ordinated and failed to concentrate their pressure, and so they failed.

The French cavalry sent to attack the British squares at Waterloo were demoralised. They never attempted an impact with the face of a square, and usually advanced at a walk. They were formed in squadron columns jammed together on a narrow front. Their order was destroyed by crowding and artillery fire, their pace reduced by the slope of the ground and deep mud. Each successive squadron was impeded by the prostrate casualties of the one ahead. Having faced their square, and suffered from its fire, each squadron halted, hesitated, then wheeled left or right into the intervals of the British Line (squares in *échiquier*) to face more fire, or a counter-attack by cavalry.

Even when infantry were unsupported by cavalry, and their fire was ineffective, Lancers sometimes failed to beat them. In July 1812 at Krasnoi, a Russian force of ten battalions on the march in close column, was attacked by Murat with a cavalry corps that included Lancers and Cuirassiers, and was supported by horse artillery. The Russian troops were raw, and their fire consequently did the French no harm. But, the Russians were steady. The French bombarded them with three horse guns, and they were subjected to repeated cavalry charges, but they never broke formation, and completed a day's march intact.

It would seem that morale, discipline and order were of more importance than weapons in determining the result of a Napoleonic engagement. The matter is well summed up by Lieutenant Tomkinson:

'The enemy attacked most gallantly, but were received so coolly, and in such order, that it was impossible to succeed unless they had ridden the square down by main force. A thing never heard of. The infantry either break before the cavalry come close up, or they drive them back with their fire. It is an awful thing for infantry to see a body of cavalry riding at them at full gallop. The men in the square frequently begin to shuffle and so create some unsteadiness. This causes them to neglect their fire. The cavalry, seeing them waver, have an inducement for riding close up, and in all probability succeed in getting into the square . . . when once broken, the infantry, of course, have no chance. If steady, it is almost impossible to succeed against infantry . . .'

When sent to attack artillery in position, cavalry would normally make an approach from the rear or flanks in open column or *échelon*. They would try to approach the guns from the opposite side to the position of any enemy infantry or cavalry in support. If the enemy support was a force of cavalry, the attackers would normally advance in *échelon*, with the second element alert to meet a counter-charge.

If the cavalry were forced to make a frontal attack, they would do so in skirmish or open order. It was not important to maintain good order when attacking artillery, as guns were not susceptible to psychological or physical shock. It was important to avoid the effects of grapeshot, which became murderous at 300 metres. So the assault force would normally gallop the last 350 metres. Once in the battery the cavalry would arrange to take away the guns, or, if this was impossible, kill as many gunners,

The 2nd (Dutch) Light Horse Lancers of the Guard

Trooper in full dress, 1811-1814.

Trumpet-corporal (Brigadier-Trompette), 1813-1814.

Velite in full dress, 1811.

Trumpeter in campaign dress, 1813.

Corporal in campaign dress, Old Guard, 1812-1814.

Trooper in full dress, Young Guard, 1813-1814.

Trumpeter in campaign dress, 1813.

Lieutenant-sous-
adjutant-major in
service dress, 1812.

Trumpet-Corporal
(Brigadier-Trompette)
in Number 2 dress,
1811.

Trumpet-Major in full
dress, 1811.

Officer in full dress,
1811.

Trumpet-Major in full
dress, 1811.

Sergeant-Major
(Marechal-des-logis) in
campaign dress, Young
Guard, 1811.

Lieutenant in full dress,
transition period,
1810-1811.

drivers and draught animals as possible. They would also do as much damage as they could to the guns and equipment, smashing sponge-staves, scattering and burning powder, cutting harness, wrecking carts and so on.

In March 1814 a French force of *Chasseurs à Cheval* and Lancers came upon 18 Russian guns near St Dizier. One squadron of Chasseurs advanced at the gallop in skirmish order towards the front of the battery. At a distance of 100 metres from it they wheeled to left and right, then charged in on both flanks. At the same moment a squadron of Lancers in open order charged the front. The battery was eliminated.

Lancers had some advantage over other cavalry once in a battery. It was easier to reach a gunner lying under a gun or limber with a lance than with a sabre.

Lancers in Campaign

Lancers had an important strategic role on campaign as well as fighting as shock troops in battle. On campaign, Lancers carried out light cavalry duties. Whilst the main body of the Army, consisting of infantry, artillery and cavalry marched in columns along the roads, Lancers and other light cavalry were active on detached service.

The detachments had offensive and defensive functions. They would seek out the enemy and do what they could to hinder him by raiding outposts, seizing couriers, ambushing enemy detachments, and attacking foragers and convoys. At the same time they screened friendly forces. Screening entailed scouring the country all around the main force to prevent ambushes, and to stop enemy raids and reconnaissances. When the Army camped in open country, light cavalry would see to the field security by providing outposts.

If the enemy was in retreat after losing a battle, light cavalry and horse guns would lead the pursuit, seeking to seize defiles ahead of the enemy forces. If the enemy had won the battle, the light cavalry and horse guns would be employed in the Rear Guard to impede his pursuit.

In the event of a siege, light cavalry with the attacking forces would blockade an enemy fortress, and at night patrol the lines of entrenchments to discourage sorties by the garrison. Light cavalry in the garrison could make such sorties. If the defences were breached, light cavalry could be formed to one side of the breach to attack the enemy storming party in flank as it poured in.

In Spain, Lancers were regularly employed in anti guerilla operations. Sometimes they fought in mixed cavalry formations with Dragoons or *Chasseurs à Cheval*. At others a company of light infantry and a squadron of Lancers, perhaps with a few horse guns, could be formed into a mobile column.

The most important detachments were the Advanced Guard and the Rear Guard.

Advanced Guards usually consisted of parties of about squadron strength. They usually moved some two days march ahead of the main columns. They found and marked convenient camping sites for the main forces, looked out for the enemy, seized and held the entrances and exits of defiles, and gathered intelligence as to the terrain and the enemy. Their main aim was to prevent a surprise or ambush by the enemy, and to hinder the enemy detachments.

They carefully inspected rivers and other obstacles, and if there were time, damaged lines of communication that could favour the enemy.

If they approached a village at night, an advanced guard of Lancers would halt about 100 metres outside, remain silent, and listen. A patrol of a few men would then circumnavigate the village to reconnoitre it. If enemy troops were seen, the detachment would either observe them and steal away, or it might attack. Such an attack might be a serious affair, or merely an 'alarm', an attempt to make the enemy apprehensive and disturb his sleep. If no enemy were seen, two or three men would go into the village, capture a local, and bring him back for questioning. If all was well, they would then enter

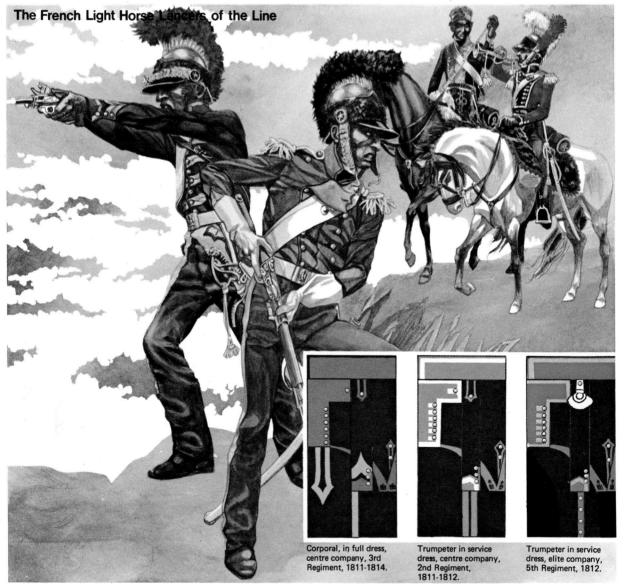

Corporal, in full dress, centre company, 3rd Regiment, 1811-1814.

Trumpeter in service dress, centre company, 2nd Regiment, 1811-1812.

Trumpeter in service dress, elite company, 5th Regiment, 1812.

Trumpet-Corporal (Brigadier-Trompette) in campaign dress, centre company, 6th Regiment, 1814-1815.

Corporal, elite company, 5th Regiment, 1813-1814.

Trooper in full dress, centre company, 2nd Regiment, 1811-1812.

Trumpeter in service dress, elite company, 4th Regiment, 1812.

Sergeant-Major
(Marechal-des-logis),
1st Regiment,
1812-1813.

Officer in walking-out
dress, 6th Regiment,
winter, 1811-1814.

Captain in full dress,
5th Regiment,
1811-1814.

Officer in service dress,
3rd Regiment, 1812.

Officer in full dress,
1st Regiment, 1811.

Officer in service dress,
4th Regiment,
1813-1814.

Officer in full dress,
2nd Regiment,
1811-1814.

the village.

If they approached a village by day, and advanced guard would send a few men forward to observe it. If the enemy were not there, a quarter of the force would enter whilst the rest remained outside. Sentries would be found from the party in the village and placed at all exits from it, and on the church tower. If the detachment decided to remain in the village for the night, it would set an 'alarm post', a rallying point in the event of attack, in the square. All roads into the village would be barricaded, with a gap left for the passage of outposts placed beyond them.

Once in a village or small town the detachment would question those of the local inhabitants who had any education, and seize all letters in the post office, all newspapers, pamphlets and other documents containing information about the enemy. If the countryside was unfamiliar, guides would be impressed from the local population. If the people were hostile the mayor and other local leaders would be held hostage until the troopers left.

Advanced Guards often provided for the lines of communication between the widely dispersed corps of an army. This was especially the case in Russia in 1812 where whole brigades of light cavalry patrolled the ground between Armies and kept them in touch with each other.

If an Advanced Guard was required to furnish information on a specific point, it would mount a reconnaissance. A reconnaissance could gain the information by stealth and observation or by attack; if by attack the force required would be larger. Once the requisite information had been gained, a reconnaissance force would usually feel free to attack and alarm enemy troops so long as it could be sure of a safe return to the main army.

On its approach march, a reconnaissance force, usually about 50 to 60 men, would try to remain undetected. It moved slowly in enclosed country. Open country was traversed as swiftly as possible, and preferably at night. Villages and crossroads were avoided. The force would move in silence in single file with an advanced guard of ten men and an NCO ten metres ahead of the main body, and a rear guard of four men and an NCO 30 metres behind. If the enemy were sighted, the whole force would take cover, then send two or three men forward to observe. Enemy couriers and small detachments would be attacked if silence could be preserved. Sometimes a Staff Officer could be ambushed and searched for his papers.

When retiring after a reconnaissance, the force would return to base by a different route to that of the advance. An advanced guard of 12 men and an officer would be 120 metres ahead of the main body, another officer would lead a rear guard of 25 men 120 metres behind.

Lancers might also provide the Rear Guard. When the Army was advancing this detachment would send out reconnaissance patrols to rear and flanks, round up stragglers, and guard defiles.

When the Army was in retreat the Rear Guard would try to keep enemy forces half a days march away from the main body. In pursuit of their object they would skirmish and lay ambushes for their pursuers. They would barricade defiles, at the exits rather than the entrances, and defend the barricades to gain time. If they had no time or reserves to construct a barrier across a defile, they could form to the flank of the exit, and charge the head of any enemy column that emerged.

Ambushes could be spontaneous or calculated. A good ambush position would afford the ambushers good cover from their intended victims' line of approach. It would also have a secure and open line of retreat, and good ground in the direction of the expected enemy route. The chances of success in ambush were improved by bad weather.

In open country, Lancers often provided outposts to secure the main body of the Army whilst it was stationary. The outpost system consisted of four main elements; the Picquet, the Grand Guards, the Small Posts, and the Videttes.

The Picquet would be placed between the main body and the Grand Guards. It would have a sentry 20 metres down the way towards each of the Grand Guards. The men would be allowed to light fires and to shelter in buildings, but half the horses were kept saddled and bridled.

The Grand Guard would be placed halfway between the Picquet and the chain of Videttes, and would be of the same strength as the Picquet – perhaps a squadron or company. Half the men of the Grand Guard would be allowed to unbridle. The roles of the Grand Guard were to relieve the Videttes, and to support them and give the alarm to the Picquet and the main body, if the enemy approached.

From each Grand Guard, lines fanned out to the small posts. Each small post would consist of perhaps a dozen men commanded by an NCO. All the horses were kept permanently bridled and fires were, in theory, not allowed. At Sombref in 1815, French outposts tried to conceal their fires by lighting them in holes in the ground, but they were clearly visible to the Prussians. If a Vidette fired, the Small Post would mount; if a Vidette made a signal, the Small Post would send a few men forward as reinforcements.,

Beyond the Small Posts, but always within sight of them, were the Videttes, each consisting of one or two men. Videttes were so placed that they could see all lines of approach, and remain within sight of the next Vidette in the chain. Videttes took advantage of cover or shadows to remain concealed, remained mounted at all times, and kept carbine and pistols ready. If Videttes saw the enemy coming, they would fire to give the alarm, and commence skirmishing, supported by the small post and Grand Guard. In good clear weather and open country, Videttes would be about 500 metres apart.

Videttes were relieved every hour, small posts every four hours. At night the whole system of outposts would contract and the Videttes would be relieved more frequently. In daylight, Videttes would take post on high ground. At night they lurked in hollows, concealed and able to see anyone coming outlined against the sky.

The Picquets and Grand Guards sent out patrols of about three men. Patrols moved as silently and unobtrusively as possible, to test the vigilance of the Videttes, and to scour the ground between them. They usually moved in extended single file. If a stranger approached a Vidette, the Vidette would usually halt him until a patrol came, whereupon the stranger would come forward to be identified and taken to the rear. Reliefs were often used as patrols on their way to become Videttes. Patrols were often more useful than Videttes because movement prevented them from falling asleep.

French cavalry were often casual in their performance of outpost duties, as illustrated by two incidents, both of which occurred in Russia in October 1812.

Beyond Moscow at Spass Kouplia, a corps of cavalry, consisting of Cuirassiers and Lancers commanded by Murat was encamped in a wood. The wood gave them a sense of security, and they neglected their outposts. At dawn one moving regiment of Cossacks suddenly charged through the wood (which was quite open), and through the French bivouac, no doubt encouraged by the thought of the horseflesh and cats which were boiling away for breakfast in the mess kettles. The French fled from the wood into open ground, some on foot, some mounted, all in panic and disorder. As they emerged they were charged by Russian Cuirassiers in line and were utterly routed.

The Light Horse Lancers of Berg

Officer in full dress, Light Horse Lancers of Berg, 1810-1813.

Sergeant-Major (Marechal-des-logis) in full dress, Light Horse Lancers of Berg, 1811-1813.

Officer in Number 2 dress, Light Horse Lancers of Berg, 1810-1813.

Trumpeter in service dress, elite company, Light Horse of Berg, transition period, 1809.

Corporal in Number 2 dress, Light Horse of Berg, transition period, 1809.

Trooper in service dress, Light Horse Lancers of Berg, elite company, 1810-1813.

Corporal in campaign dress, centre company, Light Horse Lancers of Berg, 1810-1813.

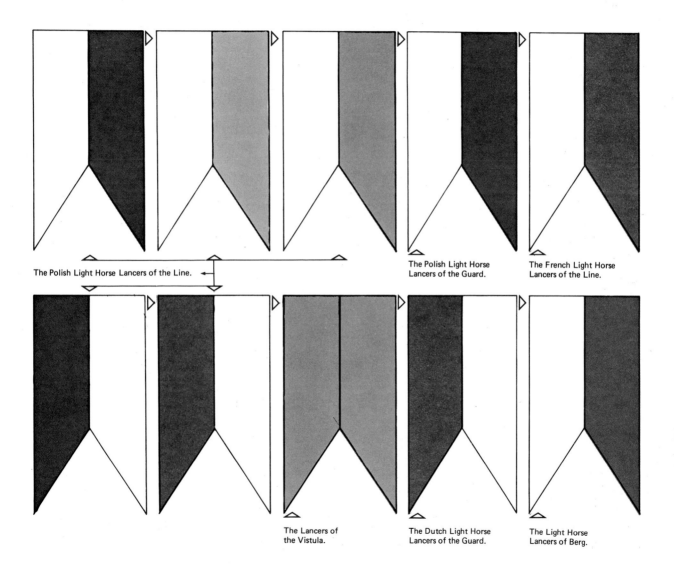

The Polish Light Horse Lancers of the Line.

The Polish Light Horse
Lancers of the Guard.

The French Light Horse
Lancers of the Line.

The Lancers of
the Vistula.

The Dutch Light Horse
Lancers of the Guard.

The Light Horse
Lancers of Berg.

Conclusions

French Lancers were not heavy cavalry, although they were often used to supplement or replace Cuirassiers as a shock force in battle, nor were they light cavalry, although on campaign they performed the same duties as Hussars and *Chasseurs à Cheval*. They were medium cavalry, adaptable, and consequently maids of all work.

The lance undoubtedly gave them an advantage in the approach and advance phases of a charge, because it had a great psychological effect. It also conferred advantages of a physical nature during the impact and pursuit phases. During the *mêlée* it was an encumbrance. A further disadvantage of Lancers was that they took longer to train; they had to learn how to use an additional weapon, and in order to use it effectively and safely had to reach a high standard of performance in evolutions and manoeuvres.

On campaign duties, the lance was of no advantage; the duties performed by Lancers were done equally well by other types of light cavalry and by Dragoons.

Bibliography

Lt Col R. H. de Montmorency – *Proposed Rules and Regulations for the Exercise and Manoeuvres of the Lance*, Longman, London, 1820.

Capt J. B. Drouville – *On the Formation of British Lancers*, Stockdale, 1813.

F. de Brack – *Light Cavalry Outposts, Recollections*, Mitchell & Co, 1876.

Capt E. Walker – *Military Elements*, Mitchell & Co, London, 1868.

Baron Jomini – *The Art of War*, Trubner, London, 1879.

Capt L. Nolan – *Cavalry; Its History and Tactics*, Bosworth, 1853.

W. Miller – *Elements of the Science of War*, Longman, London, 1811.

Sir C. W. Oman – *Studies in the Napoleonic Wars*, Medway, London, 1929.

Gen. Sir E. Wood – *Achievements of Cavalry*, Bell, London, 1897

Lt. Col. G. T. Denison – *History of Cavalry*, Macmillan, London, 1877.

H. Lachouque & A. S. K. Brown – *The Anatomy of Glory*, Brown University, California, 1962.

D. G. Chandler – *The Campaigns of Napoleon*, Weidenfeld, London, 1967.

Anglesey – *A History of the British Cavalry*, Lee Cooper, London, 1973.

Col H. C. B. Rogers – *Napoleon's Army*, Purnell, London, 1974.

F. Masson – *Cavaliers de Napoleon*, Paris, 1902.

H. Houssaye – *1815, Waterloo*, Adam & Charles Black, London 1900.

Maj Gen H. T. Siborne – *Waterloo Letters*, Cassell, London 1891

W. Siborne – *The Waterloo Campaign of 1815*, Constable, London 1895.

Sir E. Wood – *Cavalry in the Waterloo Campaign*, Sampson & Low, London, 1895.

Col G. Cathcart – *Commentaries on the War in Russia and Germany in 1812 and 1813*, Murray, London, 1850.

E. Foord – *Napoleon's Russian Campaign of 1812*, Hutchinson, 1914.

Gen Sir R. Wilson – *The Invasion of Russia*, Murray, London, 1860.

Gen Sir R. Wilson – *Private Diary (Ed. H. Randolph)*, Murray, London, 1861.

Lt. Col. W. Tomkinson – *Diary of a Cavalry Officer*, Swan Sonnenschein, London, 1860.